Soul Waves

Verses from the Deep

Akanksha

BookLeaf Publishing

India | USA | UK

Copyright © Akanksha
All Rights Reserved.

This book has been self-published with all reasonable efforts taken to make the material error-free by the author. No part of this book shall be used, reproduced in any manner whatsoever without written permission from the author, except in the case of brief quotations embodied in critical articles and reviews.

The Author of this book is solely responsible and liable for its content including but not limited to the views, representations, descriptions, statements, information, opinions, and references ["Content"]. The Content of this book shall not constitute or be construed or deemed to reflect the opinion or expression of the Publisher or Editor. Neither the Publisher nor Editor endorse or approve the Content of this book or guarantee the reliability, accuracy, or completeness of the Content published herein and do not make any representations or warranties of any kind, express or implied, including but not limited to the implied warranties of merchantability, fitness for a particular purpose.

The Publisher and Editor shall not be liable whatsoever...

Made with ❤ on the BookLeaf Publishing Platform
www.bookleafpub.in
www.bookleafpub.com

Dedication

"Dedicated to the reader who finds these lines
meaningful."

Preface

Poetry has been a part of me for as long as I can remember. As a child, I would scribble down verses in the corners of my notebooks, unaware that those little fragments of thought would one day become the foundation of my dreams. Being an introvert, words became my escape, my way of giving life to emotions that were too deep for ordinary conversation. I found comfort in poetry, in the way it could capture unspoken feelings, transform silence into meaning, and make even the most fleeting moments last forever.

Growing up, my inspiration came from everywhere — society, the changing seasons of life, and my own personal experiences. I wrote about the things I saw, the emotions I felt, and the lessons life whispered to me. I always had a vision in my heart that one day I would publish my poetry and share it with the world. But as time passed, that dream slowly faded into the background. One glad moment as a poet was when one of my poems received a **state-level award**. That recognition was a sign that my words had meaning beyond just my personal emotions. They had the power to touch others, to resonate with people in ways I never imagined. It was a moment of validation and a glimpse of what could be if I continued to follow my passion. But despite this achievement, life moved forward, and so did I. Away from the world of poetry, I was soon lost in the rush of responsibilities.

Life got busy. My studies, my career, and the responsibilities of adulthood pulled me in different directions. The blank pages of my notebook remained untouched and the words that once flowed so effortlessly became distant memories. I told myself that I would return to writing when I had more time or when life became less demanding. But somehow, that time never came. Days turned into years, and before I realised it, poetry had become a forgotten part of who I was.

Then, something unexpected happened. The world came to a halt during the COVID-19 lockdown. In the stillness of those days, **my brother, Aman**, reminded me of the poet I used to be. He encouraged me to start writing again, to find my voice, to return to the words that had once given me so much joy. But by then, self-doubt had settled deep within me. I hesitated, questioning whether I still had the ability to write, whether my poetry still had meaning. It's strange how we can lose confidence in something that once felt like second nature.

For a while, I struggled to find my rhythm again. But

then, life gave me another blessing — **my husband, Vikash Srivastava.** After our marriage, he became my biggest supporter, my strongest pillar of strength. He saw something in me that I had stopped seeing in myself. He reminded me that my dreams were still alive, waiting for me to embrace them again. His belief in me was unwavering, even when I doubted myself. With his encouragement, I finally gathered the courage to take this step to turn my long-lost dream into reality.

And so, this book was born.

This is not just a collection of poems, but it is a reflection of my journey. It is about losing and finding myself again, about love and heartbreak, about hope and despair, about all the emotions that make us human. Every poem within these pages carries a part of my soul, a piece of my story, a whisper of my past and a heartbeat of my present.

I believe poetry is about the poet including the reader who finds themselves within the words. It is about connection, about emotions that transcend time and space, about the silent comfort of knowing that someone, somewhere, understands what you feel.

As you turn these pages, I hope you find words that

resonate with your heart, emotions that mirror your own, and verses that make you pause, reflect, and feel deeply. I hope this book becomes more than just a collection of poetry for you. I hope it becomes an experience, a journey of emotions, a companion for the moments when you need words to hold on to.

So, take a deep breath, step into this world of poetry, and let my words speak to you. Let them comfort you, inspire you, and remind you that you are never alone in what you feel.

With love, gratitude, and poetry,
Akanksha

Acknowledgements

This book is not just a collection of poems, but it is a piece of my soul, a journey through emotions, memories, and dreams that have finally found their voice. however no journey is ever walked alone, and this one would not have been possible without the love, guidance, and support of some incredible people in my life.

First and foremost, to my brother, **Aman**, who rekindled the poet in me when I had almost forgotten her existence. Thank you for your constant encouragement. During the stillness of the lockdown, your words became the push I needed to start writing again. You reminded me of the passion I had set aside, and I will always be grateful for that.

I express my deepest gratitude to my husband, **Vikash Srivastava**. He has been my rock, my greatest encourager, and the one who believed in me even when I doubted myself. His unwavering support, love, and motivation gave me the strength to take this leap and turn my dream into reality. Without him, this book might have remained just a thought in the back of my mind.

A heartfelt thank you to my parents, **Reeta Sinha** and **Sunil Kumar Sinha 'Mukul'**, who shaped me into the person I am today. Their unconditional love, sacrifices, and values have given me the strength to chase my dreams. They taught me the power of words, the importance of resilience, and the beauty of emotions. Every achievement of mine is a tribute to their endless support and blessings.

To my **friends**, who have walked beside me through the ups and downs of life. Thank you for shaping my emotions, for being a part of my laughter and tears, for listening to my words long before they found a place in this book. Your presence in my life has given me stories to tell, emotions to express, and a heart full of gratitude.

And to you, **my dear reader** — thank you for picking up this book and allowing my words to reach you. Poetry is a bridge between hearts, and if even one poem in this collection resonates with you, makes you feel seen, understood, or less alone, then my purpose as a poet is fulfilled.

Lastly, I thank **life** itself for every experience, every emotion, and every lesson that has shaped my poetry. Writing has been my refuge, my way of making sense of the world, and I am beyond grateful to be able to share this journey with you.

With love, gratitude, and poetry,
Akanksha

1. Blessings

O Lord Ganesha, remover of all obstacles...
I stand before you with hands folded...
My heart full of hope and trust...
At the doorway of a path unknown.
Let my words shape my destiny...
Let my stories reveal my soul.
Hold me in your gentle hands...
Lift me beyond fear, beyond doubt, into light.
Let my thoughts flow like a sacred river...
Free, fearless, and full of life.
Let wisdom shine within me like a lamp...
And strength steady my every step.
O Ganesha, I bow to you with gratitude—
For this life, this breath, this moment...
For the gift of creation, the power of words...
For the voice you have given me.
With every word, I offer my heart...
A whisper of devotion inked with love.
Bless me with the sight to see beyond...
With the courage to write my deepest truths...

May my words be a light in the dark...
A bridge between souls, a song of your love.
Guide me when silence weighs heavy...
When doubts creep in, when my voice shakes.
And when words pour from my heart...
Let me always remember your grace.
O Lord, let gratitude be my guide...
For I walk this path with you beside me.
In every verse, in every untold story...
Let my pen dance to your endless blessings.

2. The Light Within

I have walked through storms, so wild and vast...
Where dreams I cherished shattered fast.
I gave my all, my heart, my soul...
Yet life rewrote my every goal.

I watched my wishes slip away...
Like sand that winds just steal and sway.
For years, my lips forgot to smile...
As sorrow walked with me each mile.

My silence echoed in the air...
Yet no one saw the pain I bear.
They called me rude, they called me proud...
But I was lost within the crowd.

An introvert with words unsaid...
A heart that silently had bled.
Day by day criticism cut me deep...
Yet still, my strength I swore to keep.

And through it all, what held me tight...
What turned my darkness into light.
Was 'hope' — a whisper, soft yet strong...
That told me pain won't last too long.

It held my hand through endless night...
And filled my soul with quiet might.
It taught me storms don't break, but bend...
And every wound will someday mend.

With every scar, I rose anew...
A phoenix kissed by morning's dew.
The world may judge, may never see...
But hope has always carried me...

So here I stand, with lessons deep...
A past that tried but couldn't keep.
For hope remains, my light, my guide...
Forever shining by my side.

3. Confessions of an Introvert

I love my peace, my quiet space...
Avoiding people — just in case..!
A ringing phone? Oh, what a scare...
I'd rather act like I'm not there..!

A party invite makes me sweat...
"Oh no, not socialising yet..!"
I grab my mobile, I clutch my head...
"Sorry, I'm sick. I'll stay in bed."

Small talk feels so weird, so fake...
Why must I smile for conversation's sake..?
Or worse— discussing rain or shine...
I smile and wish they'd skip this line..!

Crowds and noise? No, thanks, I'm good..!
I'd rather be in my own hood.
But oh, happiness— I won't explain...
Watching movies alone? Best kind of escape..!

And oh, the joy of solo trips—
No arguments, no travel tips...
No waiting up, no plans to keep...
Just me, the road, and a dream so deep..!

Group projects? My personal hell...
Just text me, that will do as well..!
I'll do the work, don't call, don't meet...
Let's keep this friendship short and sweet.

Yet people say, "Oh, you're so rude..!"
Nah, my dear, I'm just subdued.
I love my space, I love my time.
Solitude? It's just sublime..!

My friends complain, "You never show..!"
Well, Netflix needs me, don't you know..?
A cosy couch, a book, some tea—
That's the perfect time for me..!

So don't mistake my silent art...
I have a loud and loving heart..!
It's not you, no, it's really me...
An introvert, and proud to be..!

4. Love Across Dimensions

In the matrix of time, where particles twirl,
Our moments aligned, now drift in a whirl.
Two souls in superposition, worlds apart,
Waves of our love collapse, a fractured heart.

Like Schrödinger's fate, love lived and died,
Both real and unreal, till the box pried.
We spun like quarks in a cosmic embrace,
Yet uncertainty kept shifting our place.

Entangled we were, no distance could break,
A force unseen, yet too strong to shake.
But like photons split, scattered through space,
We chase reflections, yet never embrace.

Our timeline split, a divergent stream,
Yet echoes remain in the fabric between.
Collapsing probabilities, rewriting fate,
Still searching for you beyond the gate.

Across dimensions, I reach through the void,
Hoping for a quantum leap to where we're not
destroyed.
Yet in this universe, our love is a faded hue,
Living in a parallel universe, I feel entangled with you.

5. Thread of Life

Life is fragile, a thread so thin,
A fleeting breath, where dreams begin.
A story written in silent sighs,
Yet left untold beneath the skies.
Like ocean tides, we rise and fall,
Passing moments, yet we crave them all.

We rise, we fall, we break, we bend,
Chasing roads that never end.
Hope flickers like a distant star,
Close enough, yet still so far.
Hope flickers like a distant star,
Close enough, yet still so far.

Love—the force that shapes our days,
A quiet fire, a guiding blaze.
It heals, it scars, it makes us whole,
A whispered promise to the soul.
We give, we lose, we learn, we ache,
Yet somehow love is worth the break.

Ambition drives with restless hands,
Building castles in the sands.
We run, we push, we fight, we climb,
Believing worth is earned with time.
Yet in the chase, we lose our way,
Forgetting to live along the way.

Success—a shadow, gold yet gray,
A prize that fades as dreams decay.
We grasp at it with hungry hands,
Yet watch it slip like shifting sands.
And when we have it, all we see—
It never filled the void in me.

In moments quiet, stripped of pride,
We seek for truths we hold inside.
Not in power, nor in gain,
But in surrender, we break the chain.
Happiness was never in the race,
But in the love, the pause, the grace.

So we walk, hearts scarred yet strong,
Through joy, through pain, we move along.
And in the end, we learn to see,
That life's true gift is simply to be.

For love and loss, success and pain,
Are threads that weave us whole again.

11

6. Unbreakable

She walks with quiet grace, yet stands so tall...
A fortress of wisdom, never to fall.
Her voice, a melody, calm and wise...
A guiding star in stormy skies.

She sees the world with a scholar's mind...
No puzzle too great, no truth confined.
Her words—like rivers, deep and vast...
Lessons of life that forever last.

She plays the game before it's begun...
A queen on the board, outthinking everyone.
Yet her heart is soft, her touch so light...
A hand to hold in the darkest night.

She crafted warmth in every meal...
Each bite a love I still can feel.
Her kitchen, a place where stories unfold...
Tales of courage, wisdom untold.

She taught me to swing, to play, to fight...
To chase the ball, to aim for flight.
In cricket's crease, in table tennis' spin...
She made me believe I could always win.

Through every storm, she stayed so strong...
Even when life had done her wrong.
No tear would fall, no fear would show...
Yet her love taught me all I know.

She holds a mind both vast and rare...
With talents woven fine and fair.
She paints, she solves, she leads with ease...
Yet asks for nothing, just hopes to please.

She could outshine the brightest light...
With quiet strength and silent might.
But still she bows, so full of grace...
A humble soul in a brilliant place.

I am strong because she stood so tall...
Because she never let me fall.
Her gene runs deep within my soul...
Her spirit—the force that keeps me whole.

I am strong because she showed me how...
With fearless steps and a head unbowed.

Call her a warrior, a genius, a sage...
But to me, my **'mother'** is beyond any page.

14

7. Beyond the Flag

You blame the government.
You say the system is broken.
You raise your voice in frustration,
as if shouting will fix everything.

But tell me...
when was the last time you did something for your
country
without anyone watching?

You ask for your rights.
You demand them.
But do you even remember
that you also have fundamental duties?
Do those words mean anything to you?
Or are they just lines in a forgotten civics book?

You want a job,
but you never tried to learn a skill.
You didn't study.

You didn't prepare.
You failed your own efforts,
and still blamed the nation for failing you.

You throw garbage on the street,
and then complain the country is filthy.
You expect Swachh Bharat
but don't pick up your own waste.
Cleanliness isn't a campaign—
it's a responsibility.

You raise the flag on Republic Day,
sing the anthem on Independence Day,
and then fold your patriotism back into a drawer
until the next India-Pakistan match.

You mock your own traditions,
laugh at your own languages,
and call other countries "better."
When did being Indian
start feeling like not enough?

India isn't perfect—
no country is.
But it breathes through its people.
And right now,
it's gasping.

Do you know what it means to love your country
when no one is watching?
It means doing the right thing
when there's no reward,
no camera,
no applause.

It means knowing your fundamental duties
and still doing more.
Because this land—
this soil—
is not just a place on a map.
It's your identity.

So the question isn't what the country gave you.
The question is—
what have you given back?

8. The Unconditional One

It wasn't a spark, nor love at first sight,
No magic, no pull, no stars shining bright.
No whispered fate, no destined call,
Just time unfolding—that was all.

Yet kindness wove its quiet thread,
A bond unspoken, softly spread.
Through every moment, every care,
A love was planted, unaware.

And so it grew, not loud, but deep,
A vow unspoken, a trust to keep.
Not built on passion, wild and free,
But quiet acts of loyalty.

Then love stepped forth, a hand held out,
A voice so sure, devoid of doubt.
"Forever," it asked, so pure, so true,
Yet one heart hesitated—unsure what to do.

Dreams were vast, the world was wide,
Love was a door, not a guide.
Yet love stood still, it did not leave,
It stayed, it cared, it dared to believe.

Time moved on, and hearts aligned,
Promises made, futures designed.
Years went by, love deepened more,
A quiet fire at its core.

But love that's blind will never see
The signs that whisper, "set it free."
For when the heart has given all,
It doesn't hear the warning call.

Then one day, the truth was clear,
A secret whispered close to fear.
Lies wrapped in the softest tone,
Love had never been alone.

Questions asked, but answers cold,
Love stood distant, harsh, and bold.
No guilt, no shame, no tear to shed,
Just empty words and silence instead.

Yet still, belief refused to break,
Still hoping love would mend mistakes.

Through every wound, through every scar,
Still reaching for what once felt far.

Years kept passing, lost in wait,
While love kept building higher gates.
Pleas unheard as time slipped by,
A fading glow, a darkened sky.

"You bring me darkness," love would say,
Yet love had taken the light away.
Dreams once golden, bold and vast,
Were shadows now of what had passed.

Still, the heart stayed, still it tried,
Still it hoped, though love had died.
Not for gifts, not for gain,
Not for joy, not for pain.

It asked for nothing, not even love,
Only to be enough.
Yet love, so cruel, so blind, so small,
Gave nothing back, gave nothing at all.

And then, at last, it walked away,
Love that never meant to stay.
Not with grace, not with care,
Just empty hands, just vacant air.

And yet, though love had turned to dust,
The heart that gave still learned to trust.
For love is not what holds one down,
But what remains when none's around.

No longer waiting, no more chains,
No more pleading, no more pain.
Love was never meant to be
A war one fights to set it free.

So the heart that bled now softly mends,
For love that's real, it never ends.
Not in the arms that chose to leave,
But in the strength to finally breathe.

For love was never loss or shame,
But in the light one dares to claim.
Not in the hands that let it go,
But in the strength to rise and grow.

For love that's true will never weigh
The cost it bears, the price it pays.
It smiles through tears, through endless night,
And fades to dust—a soul's last light.

Sometimes love means setting free,

Choosing their joy over "you and me."
Not every love is meant to stay,
But true love lets go the hardest way.

If the love asked for life itself,
The heart would give with silent wealth.
Not for glory, not for pride,
But for unconditional love—side by side.

9. A Glowing Life

The sun still rises, bold and bright,
Chasing away the lonely night.
A golden promise, warm and new,
Whispering, "Dreams still wait for you."

The past is gone, it taught, it stung,
Yet here you stand—alive, so young.
Not in the years, but in your soul,
A heart unbroken, brave and whole.

Let laughter bloom like fields of spring,
Let every breath be birds that sing.
The storms may roar, the winds may call,
But light will always rise through all.

A thousand steps, a million tries,
Each fall is just a new sunrise.
You're more than pain, you're more than fears,
You shine beyond the wasted tears.

So dance with hope, embrace the day,
Love will forever light the way.
For life's a gift, a fleeting art—
Live it loud. Live with your heart.

10. Boundless

We fought like warriors, just you and me...
We were just kids, wild and free.
Our games, our rules, we made them our own...
But in the silence, I always felt alone.

Bro...You were my rival, my constant fight...
The one who tested me day and night.
But in every clash, in every tear...
I always knew you were so near.

I left for a world that was far from home...
A hostel, a place where I'd roam alone.
But each visit home, I felt something shift...
A bond growing strong, a precious gift.

When did you become my heart's own guide?
When did I stop pushing you aside?
When did you become my closest friend?
When did our journey together begin to blend?

We talk of worlds, of stars and light...
Of quantum truths that set us alight.
Hours spent in wonder, lost in thought...
Sharing dreams we'd never have sought.

We talked about the craziest thoughts...
Ideas and dreams that time forgot.
You're the one I turn to when skies are gray...
You're my laughter, my joy, my stay.

You are my support, my endless guide...
The one who's always by my side.
In the deepest struggles, in the darkest night...
You were my strength, my guiding light.

No longer just a sibling, no longer just a mate...
You're my best friend, and that's no debate.
From the boy I fought with, to the man I trust...
In you, I've found the friend so just.

11. The True Worship

How can you bow before the divine,
When your heart is dark, and far from fine?
You light the lamps, you chant and pray,
But does your soul truly feel that way?

You go to temples with hands raised high,
But do you ever stop to ask why?
How can love and hate live side by side,
When one should fade, the other guide?

You hurt, you judge, then turn to pray,
But what of the pain you cause each day?
How can God forgive what's left behind,
When all that's shown is a troubled mind?

God is watching your every move,
Your deeds, your actions... what you prove.
Karma is the law that guides your way,
It's in your heart, in what you say.

True worship is more than what we do,
More than rituals, more than the view.
It's in the kindness we give, the love we share,
In the way we show that we truly care.

I'm not an atheist, I have my way,
I pray with my heart, and in my own way.
Worship to me is in how I live,
In the love I give and the joy I give.

12. Echoes of a Fading Love

In stories woven through time's embrace,
Love was once a sacred space.
Sita walked through forests deep,
Her vows to Ram hers to keep.

She left behind her silken throne,
To make his exile not alone.
Through dust and dark, through storms untamed,
Her love stood strong, her soul unchained.

And when she crossed that fateful line,
A trap was set by hands unkind.
Yet Ram, with love so just and true,
Never asked, never withdrew.

He fought the world but not her choice,
For trust was more than a doubting voice.
Love was faith, unshaken, bright,
Not bound by fear, but by the light.

And Savitri, in fate's cruel test,
Fought Yama with a heart possessed.
With tears unbowed, with fearless breath,
She pulled her love back from death.

But today, where has love gone?
Where do these sacred stories belong?
Devotion fades, hearts turn cold,
Promises now are bought and sold.

Once, wives prayed for husbands' lives,
Now some conspire, the dagger thrives.
Gold and greed replace the vow,
Love is weighed in rupees now.

And men, once called protectors true,
Now wound the hearts they once pursued.
Ram stood with honour bright,
Yet dignity now fades from sight.

Some eyes now wander, hands betray,
Love is shattered, cast away.
Vows are spoken, yet mean so little,
Like empty glass—so sharp, so brittle.

Lies and whispers, cruel disdain,
Turn homes into silent pain.

The hands that once were meant to heal,
Now break the hearts they swore to shield.

The tales of faith, of love so rare,
Now linger as echoes in the air.
Yet somewhere, hope still softly burns,
For love that gives and asks no return.

For love is not in wealth or name,
Not in power, not in fame.
It is in the hands that truly stay,
Through storms, through tears, through darkened days.

So may the past not fade in vain,
May love find strength to rise again.
Let honesty and kindness shine,
And make this world a place divine.

13. Just Married

Before marriage, life was chill,
Woke up at noon, paid my bills.
No pressure, no rules, no fuss,
Then...BAM!... Marriage hit like a bus!

I stepped in, all smiles and grace,
Determined to be *sanskaar ki face*!
Nobody asked me to change a thing,
But my own brain started to sing.

"Wake up early, cook with flair!"
But the kitchen? A nightmare lair!
Tried making *roti*, soft and round,
It flew off the pan... never to be found!

"Do some pooja, ring the bell!"
But I mixed prasad with chili as well.
Folded my hands, tried to pray,
Forgot the mantra—Oops, what to say?!

Then came the saree—graceful, neat...
Until I walked... hello, tangled feet!
Pinned it tight, stood with pride,
Took one step—splat!—on my side!

Guests arrived—I ran like a deer,
"Serve them tea, look sincere!"
Tray in hand, I tried my best,
Spilled it all—hot mess, impressed?

But surprise! No judging eyes,
Just laughter, love, and warm replies.
Turns out, no one told me to change,
It was just me—acting deranged!

My in-laws laughed, my husband sighed,
"Be yourself, we're on your side!"
So, sanskaari? Maybe not quite,
But the house is fun, and the vibe is right!

No perfect bahu, but hey...! I try,
And at least I make them laugh (and not cry)!
No perfect bahu, no five-star meals,
But at least I bring comedy feels!

14. The Loudest Laugh

They say, "You're always so full of light,
Always laughing, always bright."
They think I'm fine, they think I'm free,
But they don't know what's inside of me.

They say the ones who laugh the most
Could never know what it's like to be lost.
They laugh, they shine, they play along...
How could they break? They look so strong.

I joke, I smile, I play along,
I make them laugh, I sing their song.
But when the crowd has gone away...
I break in ways I cannot say.

They don't see me late at night...
Staring at the ceiling, losing the fight.
They don't hear the thoughts I hide...
The ones that whisper, "You're not alright."

The echoes die, the mask comes down...
The weight of silence drags me down.
A thousand jokes, a million grins,
Yet no one sees the war within.

Because if I'm smiling, I must be okay...
If I make them laugh, then I'll be okay.
But the truth is heavy, it drags me deep...
I laugh all day, but I cry to sleep.

So don't believe the mask you see...
The happiest face might not be free.
Sometimes the loudest laugh in the room...
Is hiding the deepest kind of gloom.

15. The Love That Found Me

I never thought love was meant for me
I built my walls, I let things be.
They said, "Marriage will change your life"
But all I felt was fear and strife.

I had spent my years on my own,
The words unsheared, a life alone.
How could I share my days, my space?
How could I love in a stranger's place?

But then, there was you—so warm, so kind,
With gentle hands and an open mind.
You didn't push, you didn't demand,
You just stood there, held my hand.

You saw the weight I tried to hide,
The battles fought so deep inside.
You never judged, you never ran,
You simply said, "I understand."

You taught me love is not a chain,
Not built on fear, not built on pain.
It's in the little things you do,
The quiet ways you say, "I'm here for you."

You listened when my words ran dry,
You stayed when all I did was sigh.
You laughed with me, wiped my tears,
Held me close through all my fears.

You never asked me to change my ways,
You simply lit the darkened days.
You gave me space, you let me grow,
With every smile, you let me know—

That love is patient, love is free,
Love is knowing you stand with me.
I once feared marriage, but now I see,
I wasn't trapped—your love set me free.

16. Worth

Have you ever felt like a fading light,
Dimming slow in the dead of night?
Like hands keep reaching to smother your spark,
Turning your dawn into endless dark?

Have you ever felt like you don't belong,
Like no one listens, like everyone's wrong?
They talk over you, they push you aside,
Like your thoughts don't matter, like you should hide.

Have you ever felt like you're never enough,
No matter how hard, no matter how tough?
You give your best, yet they still complain,
Like your effort is wasted, like it's all in vain.

Have you ever felt like a whispered name,
Spoken only in passing shame?
Like every glance is a loaded gun,
Firing words that make you run?

Have you ever felt like a price tag worn,
Ripped and tattered, used and torn?
Like they name your worth in hollow lies,
As if your value is theirs to decide?

Have you ever felt like a burden to bear,
Like no one would notice if you weren't there?
You smile, you laugh, you play along,
But inside, it feels like you're barely strong.

Have you ever felt like they take too much,
Your kindness, your time, your gentle touch?
And when you need someone to see your pain,
They turn away, they leave you again.

Have you ever felt like you're fighting alone,
Every battle cuts to the bone?
Like the world is set on making you small,
So why stand tall—why stand at all?

But listen—just stop, don't let them decide,
Your worth is real, don't push it aside.
If they try to break you, don't help them win,
Stand for yourself—don't join in.

And if the weight feels too much to bear,
If the world is heavy, if no one's there,

Don't be afraid to ask for a hand,
To seek some light, to take a stand.

Therapy isn't weakness, nor is pain a crime,
Healing takes courage, it takes time.
You don't have to fight this battle alone,
There's love, there's hope—you're not on your own.

You are enough, just as you are,
No need to shrink, no need to scar.
The world may doubt you, may tear you apart,
But don't lose yourself—hold on to your heart.

17. Lost

I'm no longer afraid of what's ahead...
Just a quiet stillness in my stead.
I smile, but the joy has slipped away...
A gentle numbness clouds my day.

Life moves forward, but I've lost the spark...
Wandering through the light, stuck in the dark.
I laugh, but it's just a fleeting sound...
As I search for meaning that can't be found.

Memories whisper like autumn leaves...
Drifting past, but none relieve.
I reach for warmth, but it turns to air...
The world moves on, unaware.

Faces pass, their voices blend...
Yet nothing feels like it can mend.
Conversations fade, just hollow noise...
A crowded room, but no real voice.

The dreams I chased now feel so small...
Like distant echoes I can't recall.
The things I loved, the hopes I knew...
Now feel like stories that can't be true.

But somewhere deep, beyond the pain...
Beyond the loss, beyond the rain...
A tiny ember fights to glow...
A quiet whisper—"don't let go."

Maybe the meaning isn't clear...
Maybe the path won't just appear.
But step by step, through dark and doubt...
I'll learn what life is all about.

For even a sun that sets so low...
Will rise again, with light to show.
And maybe I, though bruised and torn...
Will find a way to be reborn.

18. Identity

I once believed a person's worth
Was shaped by jobs, their place on earth.
By where they worked, the post they held,
By papers framed and stories spelled.

I thought success was built on fame,
On wealth, on status, on a name.
That being known, being praised,
Was the only way to be truly raised.

I assumed identity could belong
To someone rich, to someone strong.
That who they knew and where they stood
Defined if they were bad or good.

But then I saw—how wrong was I!
Jobs can change, titles can lie.
Degrees fade, fame won't stay,
Money and power drift away.

A real identity is deep inside,
Not in a badge, not in pride.
It's how they love, the way they care,
The truth they speak, the pain they bear.

It's in their kindness, the way they stand,
How they help with an open hand.
It's in their heart, it's in their soul,
Not in the ranks, not in control.

But more than that, I've come to see,
Identity is in the choices we keep.
It's in the moments we rise or fall,
The paths we take, the way we call.

Do we choose truth or turn away?
Do we fight for right or let it stray?
Do we stand tall when the world is wrong?
Or do we stay silent, just move along?

For in the end, when time is done,
No one asks what race you've won.
They'll remember the love, the words you said,
Not the titles that once were read.

So now I see, and now I know,
A person's worth is in their glow.

Not in what they seem to be,
But in the love they leave in 'you and me'.

45

19. Be the Kindness

You never know what someone hides,
Behind their smile, behind their eyes.
The loudest laugh, the brightest face,
Might be the one who feels out of place.

You don't see the battles they fight inside,
The silent screams, the tears they cried.
So be the hand that doesn't let go,
The light that melts the heavy snow.

You don't know the story behind their eyes,
The dreams that broke, the countless goodbyes.
The scars they cover, the tears they blink,
Standing on edges you'd never think.

You never know the pain they bear,
The silent cries, the deep despair.
They walk among us, day by day,
Hoping someone will ask, "Are you okay?"

One small word, one gentle touch,
Might not seem like it means that much.
But to a heart that's barely holding tight,
It could be the spark that brings back light.

So be the warmth in a world so cold,
A love that heals, a hand to hold.
It costs you nothing to be kind,
But it could save a troubled mind.

Because kindness lingers, it never fades,
It echoes on in endless waves.
A simple act, a moment true—
Could be the reason someone gets through.

20. The End Of Kalyug

The world is changing, can't you see?
Nothing is real, just fantasy.
Thousands of friends, millions of fans,
Yet no one cares, no one stands.

Smiles in pictures, hearts on a screen,
But in real life, they're nowhere to be seen.
They cheer for you when you shine so bright,
But vanish fast in your darkest night.

Love is empty, just words we say,
No meaning, no feeling, all fade away.
A game we play, a mask we wear,
No one loves, no one cares.

The media whispers, the people obey,
Truth is lost in what they say.
They choose the heroes, they build the lies,
And the world believes with blinded eyes.

Pride has taken kindness' place,
Values erased without a trace.
Respect is weak, ego is strong,
No one thinks they could be wrong.

Taking a life is easier than before,
No guilt, no sorrow, just settle the score.
Children laugh while others cry,
Bullying seen as something to try.

Money decides what a person's worth,
Not talent, not effort, not honest work.
Laws are written, but who obeys?
Rules are broken in clever ways.

This is the world we've built today,
Lost in greed, led astray.
Yet even in darkness, hope can grow,
But only if we choose to know.

For one day, illusions will fade away,
And truth will rise to light the way.
But will we wake up before it's too late,
Or watch as we crumble under our fate?

21. The Night

When the sun bows low and fades from sight...
A hush descends—a world in white.
The sky unfolds in velvet deep...
Where stars like secrets softly weep.

The night, it calls with open arms...
A quiet realm of endless charms.
No voices loud, no weight to bear...
Just gentle winds that kiss the air.

The cool breeze hums a lullaby...
A soothing song, a whispered sigh.
It strokes my soul, it mends my mind...
In night's embrace, I peace do find.

Thoughts like rivers start to flow...
A world of dreams begins to glow.
Lines take form, and words take flight...
My heart spills ink beneath the night.

No fears remain, no battles fight...
I breathe, I heal beneath moonlight.
For in the dark, I'm truly free...
The night, it brings the best of me.

Yet dawn will rise, and light will creep...
Stealing the hush where my thoughts sleep.
But night still lingers in my veins...
A quiet fire that remains.

So when the world fades into blue...
I'll find the night, it's where I grew.
For every whisper, every sigh...
The night is where my soul can fly.

22. Handle With Care

I'm like a mirror... shiny, true,
Give me respect? I'll double it for you!
But throw me shade or act unfair,
I'll snap right back... so best beware!

Mock me once? Oh...! What a thrill,
Let me show you how that must feel!
A joke on me? I'll joke on you,
Let's see how well you take it too!

It's not revenge (okay, maybe a bit),
But mostly just a reflex hit.
I know, I know...I should be wise,
Not turn into a roast surprise!

I'm an odd mix...sweet as can be,
But test my patience? Lord, you'll see!
One half sugar, one half spice,
Play it cool, and we'll be nice!

Yet deep inside, I sometimes sigh,
"Did I go too far?"...I wonder why.
Cause honestly, it's bittersweet,
Winning a fight but feeling defeat.

See, once upon a time, I heard,
Too many rude and bullying words.
I promised myself, "No more pain!"
"No insults shall be mine again!"

But not all fights deserve my fire,
Not every fool needs my entire...
Wit, sarcasm, all in play,
Maybe some things should fade away.

So now I try a brand-new trick—
I pause before I make it stick.
Will this clapback feed my soul?
Or just make me lose control?

But hey, if kindness is what you bring,
I'll lift you up like you gave me wings.
But if you throw your words like knives,
I hope you like my sweet surprise...!

23. Rising After Fall

The weight of failure, sharp and cold,
It steals your strength, it takes its toll.
Once bright dreams crumble in the dark,
Leaving you with a broken heart.

You question everything you've known,
In the silence, you feel so alone.
But in the pain, you'll start to see,
Failure is the key to setting you free.

From every wound, from every scar,
You'll find the strength to go that far.
Through the ashes, a fire will burn,
A heart reborn, a soul to return.

Rise again, though bruised and torn,
Far from the night, a new hope is born.
Keep walking through the doubt and fear,
For in the end, your strength is near.

24. Illusion

They paint a picture, bright and grand...
A flawless world, so well-planned.
But behind the glow, the cracks appear...
A hidden truth we're taught to fear.

A perfect face, a polished smile...
Yet heavy hearts walk every mile.
They chase an image, never real...
A hollow dream they're forced to feel.

Perfection whispers, calls your name...
But leaves you lost inside its game.
No room for flaws, no space for doubt...
Yet silence screams when joy runs out.

But in the scars, in shattered days...
Lie strength, stories time won't erase.
Not in perfection, cold and bright...
But in the depths where souls find light.

So let them chase their fragile gold...
I'll stand with truth, imperfect, bold.
Not flawless, no, but real and free...
For in my flaws, I find all of me.

25. A Heart That Beats for India

Since childhood, a fire burned bright,
A dream to serve, to do what's right.
I teach, I help, I lend my hand,
Yet still, I long to do more for my land.

I wish for power, wealth, and might,
To lift my nation to greater heights.
But even if my reach is small,
A single spark can light it all.

I taught with heart, with pen in hand,
No grand applause, no any demand.
Just quiet hours and willing minds,
And joy in what the world now finds.

If nothing else, through all I've been,
I try to be a good citizen.
To stand with truth, to walk with pride,
With love for India deep inside.

I've picked up waste others ignore,
And held the hand of someone poor.
They may seem small, these things I do—
But they carry all my heart, it's true.

If one small deed, one step I take,
Can bring a change, a path to make,
Then blessed I'll be, my purpose true,
For India, I'll always do.

And when my final breath is gone,
May my country still march on.
No crown, no fame, just this I seek—
To see my nation strong and free.

26. Held by the Rain

When the sky turns grey and clouds roll in...
Something peaceful wakes within.
The world may worry, hide, or run...
But for me, that's when joy's begun.

The first drop falls, and I smile wide...
Like an old friend just arrived.
The noise inside me starts to fade...
As every drop clears what fear had made.

I leave my shoes, step on the ground...
No need for words, no need for sound.
Rain falls softly on my face...
And suddenly, I feel safe in this place.

I walk with no direction, no plan...
Letting rain hold my hand.
It doesn't ask why I'm feeling low...
It simply comes, and helps me glow.

Sometimes I sit on my balcony high…
Chai in hand, under a stormy sky.
Watching raindrops race on glass…
Feeling moments gently pass.

The thunder rolls—I like its voice…
Like the sky has made a fearless choice.
It doesn't scare me, it makes me feel…
That loud can also be calm and real.

The cool breeze plays with my hair…
Telling me that someone's there.
Not a person, but something kind…
A soft touch that clears my mind.

And when the rain begins to slow…
And the clouds prepare to go,
A rainbow shines, soft and wide…
A quiet hug from the sky outside.

It tells me storms don't last forever…
That dark and light can live together.
And even after heavy rain…
Something beautiful will remain.

While others run and hide away…
I thank the skies for such a day.

Because when it rains, I come alive...
My heart feels full, my thoughts survive.

So let it pour, let it stay...
I don't need the sun today.
In every drop, I find my peace...
A little more love, a little more ease.

27. The Journey to Myself

I walk like nothing's ever wrong...
Like I've been strong all along.
But behind my eyes, beneath my skin...
There's a world I rarely let you in.

You wouldn't see the battles fought...
In moments I said "I'm fine" when I was not.
You'd never guess the nights I cried...
With no one there, just pain to hide.

There are scars no one has ever touched...
Made from silence that hurt too much.
From words unsaid and warmth withdrawn...
From people who left without a dawn.

Some scars come from being too kind...
From giving when I was barely aligned.
Some from being told I wasn't enough...
Or from pretending to be someone tough.

I've been the one they leaned upon...
But had no arms when I was gone.
They cheered my smile, ignored my tears...
Praised my courage, fed my fears.

And in a world that values the loud and proud...
I kept shrinking just to not stand out.
I lost myself in trying to please...
Until I forgot I, too, had needs.

But then one day I broke in two...
No one to run to, nothing to do.
And in that mess, that shattered part...
I heard a whisper from my heart:

"You've carried too much, for far too long...
You've tried to be brave by being strong.
But strength, my love, is in being real...
In letting yourself finally feel."

So slowly, gently, I began again...
Stopped hiding sorrow, welcomed pain.
I let the tears fall when they would...
I didn't pretend to feel 'just good.'

I started to speak, though my voice would shake...
And chose myself, even if hearts would break.

I set boundaries I once feared to draw...
I let myself be weak, be raw.

I learned that healing is never fast...
And sometimes I'd still feel the past.
But every time I chose to stay...
To not give up, not to walk away.

I grew a little more, piece by piece...
Found comfort in my own release.
Started seeing my soul as a friend...
Not something broken I had to mend.

And the scars I hid? I saw them anew...
They weren't shame, they were truth.
Proof of all that I'd survived...
Of how, despite it all, I'm still alive.

Now when I look in the mirror, I see...
Not just pain...but strength in me.
A warrior made not by fight or fire...
But by standing up from sinking mire.

Loving myself is not always light...
It's holding my own hand at night.
It's knowing I'm flawed, but still enough...
Soft yet powerful, broken yet tough.

And if you too wear scars unseen...
If you smile while hiding what might've been.
Know this: you're not alone in your pain...
You too can rise again and again.

So let them talk, let them not understand...
You don't owe your soul to their demand.
Your healing is yours, your worth is too...
And no one can love you like you do.

28. Kind of Love That Heals

It didn't arrive with thunder or flame,
No grand confession, no shouting name.
It came like morning, soft and slow,
A quiet warmth I didn't know.

It didn't rush to take or claim,
It simply stayed—and stayed the same.
No questions asked, no mask to wear,
Just steady breath and honest care.

I never knew love could be this still,
A calm that bends to match your will.
It didn't ask me to be more,
It met me gently, as I wore.

There were no rules, no games to win,
Just room to breathe and let it in.
It felt like air after holding tight,
Like finally sleeping through the night.

It held no fear, no silent test,
It didn't boast, it let me rest.
It wrapped around the quiet parts,
And slowly softened hardened hearts.

I found in it a kind of peace—
Where noise would fade and doubts would cease.
No pressure to impress or prove,
Just the freedom simply to move.

It saw me, not the role I play,
Not who I was on a good day.
It saw the quiet, saw the mess—
And called it worthy nonetheless.

It cheered the tiny things I do,
It made the ordinary new.
It didn't try to paint me gold,
It just loved all that I hold.

I learned that love is not a fire,
It's not a race, it's not desire.
It's choosing someone every day,
In little words and quiet ways.

The kind of love that truly heals
Won't shout its name, but you will feel—

In how it lifts, and how it stays,
In silent strength, through fragile days.

And now I know: this love is mine—
Not loud or proud, but pure, divine.
It didn't fix me—it just stood near...
And whispered, "You're safe. I'm here."

29. Life Beyond Deadlines

They say, *"Work hard. Keep your head low.*
Hustle in silence, let your success show."
But no one speaks of the hearts that break,
Of the quiet lives we never take.

The office lights stay on till late,
The clock forgets the dinner plate.
One more task, one more call—
Another evening lost to it all.

He lives in a flat, far from home,
Scrolls through pictures when he's alone.
His mother calls, voice full of grace,
While tears roll down his tired face.

She says, *"Beta, kab aaoge ghar?"*
He lies and says, *"Soon, bas kaam ka pressure."*
But months go by, the seasons fade,
And so does the promise he never made.

The girl in HR cries in the stall,
Her mind a storm, her spirit small.
She smiles in meetings, nods along—
But inside, she knows something's wrong.

She once had dreams, she used to write,
Now she just scrolls through memes at night.
Her diary sleeps in layers of dust,
Replaced by metrics, goals, and trust—
In systems that don't see her fall,
That chase the numbers, not the call.

And founders say with puffed-up pride,
"We work Sundays too—there's no free ride."
But never mention the friends they lost,
The sleepless nights, the hidden cost.

One man collapsed at his desk last June,
He was thirty-five—he left too soon.
They said, *"Heart attack. He worked too much."*
But no one spoke of the human touch.

Birthdays missed. Anniversaries gone.
Children growing up alone.
Fathers who barely see their child,
Mothers whose laughter's no longer wild.

What are we building, if not a life?
If not time with parents, children, or wife?
A quiet meal, a deep long talk,
A moment to breathe on an evening walk.

What's the value of a pay increase,
If your soul forgets what it means to be at peace?
What's a promotion on a Monday eve,
If you've forgotten how to breathe?

So here's the truth, raw and plain:
There's more to life than profit and gain.
Success is hollow if love is gone,
If you wake up tired from dusk to dawn.

The solution? It's not in quitting it all,
But in drawing boundaries when you stall.
In learning to pause, to breathe, to feel,
In knowing that rest is also real.

Companies must lead with heart, not haste,
Not every hour should go to waste—
On chasing more at the cost of soul,
Let balance, not burnout, be the goal.

Let's rewrite what ambition means—
More sunsets, more meals, more human scenes.

A call to mom, a walk with dad,
A Sunday nap, a heart that's glad.

Work, yes—dreams are worth the flight,
But not at the cost of losing the light.
So chase your passion, climb the hill—
But live the life you're working to build.

30. Silent Goodbye

I don't want to be remembered, not in the years to
come...
No monuments rising, no battles won.
I don't seek your tears, or whispers in the night...
Just the quiet release, when I've taken flight.

Let me vanish like dusk, without a trace...
Not clinging to fame or a lasting embrace.
I don't need my name etched in stone or in rhyme...
For I've lived, and that was enough for the time.

I've no desire for echoes of what I've done...
For the world to pause, or the race to be won.
My life, like a breeze, should drift with no sound...
A soft, fading memory, lost and unbound.

I don't need to be seen in the light of your gaze...
Nor caught in your thoughts in the passing of days.
Let me be the shadow that vanishes at dawn...
Not a figure to follow, nor a name to adorn.

For love was my gift, and in it, I'll stay...
A simple, quiet heart, fading away.
I don't want the world to mourn or to sing...
Just to feel what was real, and let go of the ring.

So when I'm gone, let silence remain...
Not a cry for my memory, nor a lingering pain.
I don't want to be remembered, no legacy to keep...
Just to rest in the quiet, in peaceful sleep.

www.ingramcontent.com/pod-product-compliance
Lightning Source LLC
LaVergne TN
LVHW011046200726

843509LV00011B/1357